BITCOIN

THE NEW DIGITAL GOLD RUSH

Connor Springfield

Bitcoin – The New Digital Gold Rush

Copyright © 2017 Connor Springfield

This book is copyright protected only for personal use. You cannot amend, distribute, sell, use, quote or paraphrase any part or the content within this book without the consent of the author or copyright owner. Legal action will be pursued if this is breached.

Please note the information contained within this document is for educational and entertainment purposes only. Every attempt has been made to provide accurate, up to date and reliable, complete information. No warranties of any kind are expressed or implied. Readers acknowledge that the author is not engaging in the rendering of legal, financial, medical or professional advice.

By reading this document, the reader agrees that under no circumstances are we responsible for any losses, direct or indirect, which are incurred as a result of the use of information contained within this document, including, but not limited to, ─errors, omissions or inaccuracies.

Table of Contents

Introduction 1

Chapter 1: What are Bitcoins? 3

Chapter 2: How Bitcoin works 15

Chapter 3: How to mine Bitcoins Efficiently 20

Chapter 4: Bitcoin Exchanges 30

Chapter 5: Bitcoin real life usage 41

Chapter 6: Bitcoin Security tips and safety features 49

Chapter 7: What's next for Bitcoins and other cryptocurrencies? 57

Conclusion 63

Introduction

The digital rush sweeping the globe, and, in particular, the internet, has centered around investors of all ages and lifestyles cashing in on Bitcoin. It's the infamously unpredictable cryptocurrency that makes trading and investing as easy as sitting in front of your laptop. However, what is easy is not always simple. Part of the reason it's hard to grasp is that it has not been around for long- there is no way to truthfully psychoanalyze the comings and goings, the rises and the falls of what your currency can do. Getting involved with Bitcoin is easier and riskier than the traditional ways we think about investments. However, just like with Wall Street, there are ways to become more proficient in the art of trading and investing.

Bitcoins represent a deviation from the norm, a chance for nations to break away from the structure and bureaucracy associated with a federally mandated and controlled currency. Built from the ground up, the community and infrastructure supporting bitcoins grows larger and stronger each day, presenting an endless number of opportunities to quickly cash in on this new and exciting cryptocurrency.

As with any exchange, market, or online platform that requires a credit card, trading with Bitcoin is risky to those who are new, and those who have been working at it for quite some time. Though you probably will never hold Bitcoins in your hands, it can hurt your bottom line- you might lose real money. The most critical advice you can receive is to proceed with caution and make sure you are not pushing yourself deep into a hole.

This book will try to educate you on the options you have when it comes to trading and investing in Bitcoin. Read through before you try to start the process, make notes, and maybe sit by a prospect what is going on before you venture out on your own.

The following chapters will discuss some of the many aspects of Bitcoin and how they are used for different purposes. You are going to discover how important it is to make sure that you jump on the Bitcoin train at just the right time so that you can ensure that you are going to be capable of getting the most out of the investment that you have done.

Bitcoin prices have risen significantly and are still expected to come up in the coming years. Be prepared before the huge spike, and you will no longer be able to afford them. Among the things you will learn are the factors you should consider before investing in Bitcoin and when you are working to build up your supply of Bitcoin.

The goal of this book is to give you the necessary knowledge and strategies to successfully become wealthy by cashing in on the Bitcoin "Gold Rush" thus providing endless wealth and the ability to enjoy the finest things this world has to offer. The steps are there, the advice is clear; the money is on the table. All you require to do is read this book, follow the guidelines provided and implement the strategies.

Chapter 1:

What are Bitcoins?

Imagine a way wherein you could anonymously transfer money to anyone instantly, anywhere in the world. Someone is selling something that you want to buy, and you don't want the hassle of conveying funds from a bank account or credit card, or exchanging dollars for pounds or yens- you just want to make a secure and permanent transaction.

If you happen to have a virtual wallet full of Bitcoins you are in luck. This is so especially if those Bitcoins are more valuable now than they were when you obtained them, giving you more buying power or simply the ability to trade them for a nice sum of cash. Before we get into the nuts and bolts of how to actually make money with this unique form of currency, you will need an understanding of what Bitcoins are and how they are used. You need to know what it is that makes this anonymous currency so valuable and why people are motivated to use it for various transactions in place of many of the various world currencies in circulation.

What are Bitcoins exactly? Bitcoin is a peer-to-peer, decentralized, virtual currency which was created by a web developer called Satoshi Nakamoto. To understand the nature of this online currency, it is important to know who invented Bitcoin and why. Bitcoin is the system that Nakamoto invented, and Bitcoin is the actual unit of this virtual currency.

The idea of virtual currency has been around almost as long as the internet, providing users a way they can exchange goods and services for currency virtually instantly, without government regulation and with the ability to conduct transactions over great distances and across borders without having to exchange different currencies.

Previous forms of virtual currency had some problems, one being that they could be duplicated without value, and there was no real way to verify transactions. Nakamoto developed a system that did not suffer from these problems. Bitcoin transactions are permanent, irreversible, and somewhat anonymous helping to make them such an attractive form of currency.

Similar to gold, silver or other types of commodity-backed currency, Bitcoin has a value that is based on demand and supply. Just like gold, the supply of Bitcoins is provided by only two sources: people who already have them and people who mine them. The effort that goes into mining the Bitcoins and the Fact that there is a limited supply are both factors that contribute to the value of the Bitcoin.

Bitcoin is perhaps the final frontier when it comes to currency in different areas around the world. It is a method of payment that does not discriminate between countries, rich, poor or anything else that could identify a person. Bitcoin was created to be able to trade money terms without ever having to use the money and it is a perfect solution for the need to have something other than a typical bank for currency options. Those who use Bitcoin can understand how freeing it is to be able to rely on themselves instead of having to use the currency options that most banks have available for them.

BITCOIN

Bitcoin is a form of digital currency that is created electronically. It is not controlled by anyone. The most unique aspect of Bitcoin is that the currency is not printed like other currencies. Instead, it is produced by the solving of mathematical problems, by people all over the world. This type of currency is called cryptocurrency, and although Bitcoin is the first of its type, it is a growing phenomenon.

How different is Bitcoin from the other currencies?

Bitcoin is used to buy things online, electronically. It is like conventional euros, yen, and dollars in that way, in that they are also traded digitally. The key factor that differentiates Bitcoin from these other currencies is that it is decentralized. The bitcoin network is not controlled by a single institution. This really gives many individuals peace of mind, knowing that their money is not being managed by a large bank.

How was it created?

The idea was proposed by Satoshi Nakamoto, a software developer who proposed this payment system which is electronic and based on mathematical proof. The proposal was to create a form of money that would be independent of any central authority, and that could also be transferred electronically almost instantaneously, with little fees.

How is it printed?

A major benefit of Bitcoin is that it is not physically printed out of sight of the population, but a central bank that is making up its own rules. That system enables banks to simply print more money in order to cover the national debt, which devalues the currency. Instead, anyone can join the community of people that digitally create Bitcoin. Instead of being printed, Bitcoins are mined in a distributed network, using computing power. That same network also is responsible for processing all transactions that are made using bitcoin, which means Bitcoin is effectively its own complete payment network.

Is it not possible to churn out unlimited bitcoins?

No, that is not feasible at all. There is a limit placed by the Bitcoin protocol, of only 21 million bitcoins that can be mined. Bitcoins can be divided into smaller parts, such as the Satoshi (one hundred millionth of a bitcoin), which is named after its founder.

On what element has Bitcoin been based?

Traditional currency is based on silver or gold. Although it did not actually work in practice, when you had a dollar, in theory, you knew that if you handed it in at the bank, you could get some gold for it. However, bitcoin is based on mathematics, not gold or silver. Software programs that follow a mathematical formula which results in bitcoins are being used by people all over the world. Anyone can check this mathematical formula as it is freely available. The software is fully accessible since it is open source, which means that it can be examined by anyone.

Different aspects of Bitcoin

1. Anonymous users
   Perhaps one of the most popular aspects of Bitcoin, especially by those who used it in the early days, is the anonymity that comes with Bitcoin. While your name is technically attached to a wallet number, it's hard to show your identity when you are using Bitcoin. If you want to

be able to keep your identity secure and private, you will be able to do so with Bitcoin because of the different aspects that are included with your wallet. You are identified by a username or a wallet ID instead of being identified by your own names as you would be at a bank.

2. Physical attributes

    There are essentially no physical attributes of Bitcoin. This is because the currency is exclusively online and it is more of an idea or a series of codes than anything else. Unlike cash or credit cards, you are not able to put the Bitcoin in your wallet, and you cannot actually ever hold the currency in your hands.

3. Use

    The availability of Bitcoin in major retail locations is something that is relatively new. Many people do not actually know what Bitcoin is so it is somewhat hard for retailers to offer that as an option for the people who want to be able to use it. Because it has become increasingly popular because it is worth much more than what it once was, it has recently been featured at major retailers, like Overstock, a company that specializes in online sales and helps people who want to be able to purchase the majority of their necessities online.

    The single biggest use of Bitcoin is from one person to person. Second is from business to business and person to business or business to person comes in as the last spot for uses in the sense of entity to entity.

4. Trades between countries

    With more people getting involved in Bitcoin, it is easy for them to recognize that they will be capable of using it for many different types of transactions. In the past, businesses or individual who were in different countries had to wire money from person to person. It was complicated, and the exchange rate got in the way of being able to get the exact amount to the other party. Now with the Bitcoin, everyone who uses it around the world uses the same form of currency. There is no need for exchange rates, bank transfers or even a wait time that is sometimes needed with money that is wired.

5. Safety

    Because of the way that Bitcoin is set up, it is much safer for people to use Bitcoin and other forms of cryptocurrency than it is for them to use traditional cash or even credit cards. Bitcoin is a currency that is exclusively online. Unless your wallet gets hacked by someone who wants to get your currency, there is virtually no way to have it stolen. Even if it happens to get hacked, it is encrypted so that it can be traced exactly back to the wallet that holds the Bitcoin that was stolen from you out of your own wallet.

6. Volatile price

    The price of this electronic cash continues changing regularly. Over some time frame, the price would increment or diminish as per the market situations. It is best to not keep your funds as Bitcoins as it would lead to loads of dangers. The best thing to do is change over the digital currency quickly to your local cash. Never hold cash in this type if you can't stand to lose them.

What are the characteristics of Bitcoin?

Several important features make Bitcoin different to common currencies:

BITCOIN

- Bitcoin is decentralized
  This means that the network is not controlled by any central authority. Machines that mine Bitcoin and process the transactions work together as part of the Bitcoin network. In theory, this means that a central authority is not able to manipulate monetary policy, which would cause a collapse. It also protects the user since, unlike what happened with the central European Bank in 2013, in Cyprus, no authority can take the currency from them. The money keeps flowing even if a part of the network goes offline.
- It is entirely transparent
  Every transaction that has ever happened within the network is stored in a large electronic general ledger. This is called the Blockchain. The blockchain can tell all. Anyone is capable of telling how many bitcoins are stored at a particular bitcoin address, although they won't be able to tell who owns that address. There are ways to be less visible in Bitcoin transactions, for example, not transferring lots of bitcoin to a particular address, and not using the same Bitcoin address regularly.
- It is very easy to get set up with Bitcoin
  Opening a conventional bank account involves a lot of jumping through hoops. Setting up merchant accounts is even more difficult and complicated. In contrast, setting up a Bitcoin address takes seconds, and there is no fees payable, and no questions asked.
- Portable
  Proper currency should be able to be used in day-to-day transactions, and as such, it needs to be highly portable to carry on one's person. Currencies use as an exchange

medium is to meant to make life easier, & most individuals would not like to carry around large quantities of lead, or herding cattle to town for trade easy.

- Extremely fast

  When you send money anywhere in the world, it arrives just minutes later, immediately the payment is processed by the Bitcoin network. International transfers can cost you a $10-$30 fees from your bank. Bitcoin does not charge these fees.

- Divisible

  Few transactions in the world are for specific integer denominations. Almost each transaction has the need of making a change. This will be achieved by storing different denominations of the currency or dividing physical objects into multiple segments without any loss of value. This makes items such as art act poorly as money since they cannot be easily divided.

- Hard to Counterfeit

  In order to become a reliable store of value, the Bitcoin itself should be hard to tamper with. Recipients need to be sure that they are getting authentic items. Otherwise, they will be reluctant to use it for trade in the future.

- Non-repudiable

  Once Bitcoins have been sent, there is no return, unless the person you sent them to chooses to return them to you. Once they are gone, they are gone. Bitcoin is also anonymous that means that one can have Bitcoin addresses that are not linked to their name, address, or any other personal information.

- Widespread Use

Lastly, bitcoin should be able to be traded for a wide variety of products and services. The reliability of being able to spend Bitcoin whenever you need to do so, instead of being worried whether a merchant will accept it adds significant value.

History and the origin of the Bitcoins

As discussed earlier, the internet seemed to be ripe for the concept of digital or virtual currency almost from day one. Before Bitcoin, none of the virtual currencies appeared to last long. A group of dedicated internet users called cryptographers, those concerned with developing secure methods of making transactions over the internet in the presence of third parties, dedicated themselves to developing a stable virtual currency as early as the 1990s.

One attempt at such an anonymous currency system was made by a man named David Chaum. His currency, called ecash, relied on government and credit card company infrastructures that were already in place when he developed the system in the early 1990s. This made ecash subject to manipulation and instability that contributed to its eventual failure.

Another virtual currency emerged in the 1990s that were called DigiCash. While initially successful due to its anonymity, it eventually failed in 1998 due to partnerships with banks that disallowed the anonymity.

A system called CyberCash came onto the scene in 1994, and actually went public with a $300-million stock offering. Also attractive to users due to offered anonymity, CyberCash was initially successful but eventually filed for bankruptcy in 2001 after technical glitches that included Y2K bugs.

Meanwhile, a currency called Flooz was short lived due to its failure to provide secure transactions, including the problem of double spending. Another form of virtual currency includes those that are accumulated and spent in the virtual world such as World of War craft, Second Life, and Facebook. These virtual world currencies seem to fulfill their intended purpose but have little use outside of gaming. There are and have been others, but none as versatile as Bitcoin.

Satoshi Nakamoto published his paper in 2008 in which he detailed a new type of virtual currency that solved one problem that previous forms of virtual currency had- the problem of double spending. As mentioned earlier Bitcoin is not the first form of digital currency devised, but may be proven to be more successful than its predecessors. One of the reasons for this is that Bitcoin is not subject to double spending; that is once an individual has used a Bitcoin then it is gone, & that individual will no longer have access to it at all. Every Bitcoin is unique with its own serial number; Bitcoins cannot be duplicated or copied, and transactions are completely irreversible. Nakamoto used a system of decentralized computers that could verify each transaction and eliminate the double spending problem. In fact, it is the process of verifying transactions that the Bitcoin miners do which adds value to the system & creates new blocks of Bitcoins.

In 2011, Bitcoin became more widely known and sought after following an article by Andy Greenberg. That article, published in Forbes Magazine, described some of the attributes of the virtual currency. Subsequently, Bitcoins popularity and value soared. Many of the system users that had spent spare time verifying transactions for Bitcoin had mined and collected Bitcoins that became tremendously valuable. People began to invest in Bitcoins out of speculation, and groups of Bitcoin miners began to mine Bitcoins with the sole purpose of making money by selling mined Bitcoins.

By late 2013, Bitcoin had been valued at over US$1,000 each, presumably making many of the previous Bitcoin owners a great deal of money; this happened despite the fairly volatile US Dollar value of Bitcoin throughout that year, fluctuating by hundreds of dollars due to speculation and publicity.

In January of 2014, the total number of transaction blocks reached 210,000, and the Bitcoin reward for mining halved from 50 Bitcoins to 25 Bitcoins. Bitcoin reward for mining will remain at 25 for four years; that is until 2017, when it will divide again to 12.5 Bitcoins. Four years later, it will be reduced to 6.25 Bitcoins, and so on.

This method is automated by the software that Nakamoto devised and thus fixes the maximum amount of Bitcoins that can be generated. The Bitcoin production after each 2,016 transactions, and adjusts the difficulty of the problem solving involved in authenticating transactions to keep the rate of new Bitcoin production(mining) steady for around four years.

Currently, Bitcoins future seems uncertain, with the possibility of government regulation threatening to scare off users and investors on one hand, and encouraging investors looking for greater stability on the other hand. Two among the most trafficked Bitcoin exchanges, Mt.Gox and Bitstamp momentarily halted trading in early 2014 to work out a flaw in the public transaction ledger system that seemed to allow some users to attempt to hide, fake or even duplicate transactions. This potential threat made new and prospective users nervous, experienced users remained unfazed and bullish about the future of Bitcoin.

However, as is true with many uncertain and volatile investments, Bitcoins could prove to be an incredible money maker for those willing to do their proverbial homework and assume a certain level of risk.

Chapter 2:

How Bitcoin works

How Bitcoins Are Created, and What You Can Use Them For.

By now, one should have a fundamental understanding of why Bitcoin is valuable and why people are using them. Now, the question is, how exactly do Bitcoins work? If they're purely based online, then how are they created and what makes them worth anything? For most people who are used to traditional currency, the very idea of a digital currency can be very confusing because you can't hold something digital in your hands and you don't know where it comes from.

In this chapter, we're going to demonstrate exactly how Bitcoins are created and what gives them their worth. We're also going to explore the various ways you can use Bitcoins in your everyday life by demonstrating how they can be utilized as a means to store money, exchange money, and invest your money before moving on in subsequent chapters on the specifics of how exactly to go about purchasing and trading Bitcoins.

Bitcoin creation

Remember how gold mining works – over time it becomes more and more difficult to mine for gold. First, gold can be panned in a particular gold-producing area. This allows individuals with no startup money or even a crew to pick gold up right off the surface. As more people continuously mine for gold this way, the surface gold begins disappearing, so more advanced techniques must take place to continue producing gold such as digging into the nearby mountain.

This means that just one individual with a pickax isn't going to be able to do a very good job. So people with more capital and more equipment and a team of people come in to mine for gold and produce more of it. As time goes on, less and less gold is produced from the mountain, and it takes more and more work to dig it out because gold is a non-renewable natural resource that takes thousands of years to create.

Now, let's apply that same principle to Bitcoin. Essentially, the miner, in this case, is one individual with a computer. Back in 2009 when Bitcoin first started, an individual could download appropriate software that worked at mining Bitcoins. The software chipped away at cryptographic blocks of information by attempting to solve mathematical problems. Once a mathematical problem was solved, the person who was mining was awarded a Bitcoin.

A good way to understand this is, instead of going up and panning for gold, you were instead required to answer a riddle. If you answered the riddle correctly, you received a little bit of gold. However, as time goes on, the riddles get harder and harder to understand. After a while, you need a think tank of people who are working around the clock to solve these riddles so that they can get more gold. It's the same thing with Bitcoin.

As time has gone on, the mathematical equations that must be solved in exchange for Bitcoins just keep getting more difficult. No longer can just one person with a consumer-grade laptop install a piece of software and expect their computer to mine Bitcoins. Now you have entire operations – teams of people with super computers and specialized software designed to run 24/7 solving complex mathematical problems for more Bitcoins. They're like giant mining rigs. In fact, Bitcoin mining operations often cost thousands upon thousands of dollars to set up and maintain every month.

Currently, every 10 minutes sees the creation of 25 new Bitcoins. However, this figure is cut in half every four years, which means after 2013 12.5 Bitcoins will be created every 10 minutes and so on, and the mathematical equations that must be solved in order to mine Bitcoins will become even more complex. This will continue until the final Bitcoins are created in 2140 and only 21 Million Bitcoins will ever be in operation. This means that no centralized authority can inflate the supply and devalue the currency, and the currency will increase in value over time.

So, you see, Bitcoins are mined pretty much just like gold, except instead of using pickaxes and dynamite to mine, we're using computers and software to mine.

What Can Bitcoin Be Used For?

- Trading (Buying and Selling)
  One of the best and fastest ways to benefit from Bitcoin is through short term investment. Bitcoin prices fluctuate up and down just like stocks on the market do. It's easy for people to buy low and sell high for profit. You don't have to be some kind of financial wizard to do this, all it really takes is a discerning eye. Later we'll talk about Mt.Gox, but suffice it to say, simply keep your eye on the market. When the price of Bitcoins goes down a little – buy a few Bitcoins. Then, when they go up 10% or 20% or higher, sell

them off for a profit. Many people like to do this every couple of days to continuously profit from Bitcoin on a short-term time scale. You'll often see people buying $1,000 worth of Bitcoins at the beginning of the week and selling them at the end of the week for $1,700. It's a great way to make extra money on the side, or if you're really serious, you can even choose to do this full time.

- Quick Money Exchange
  You don't have to use Bitcoin as an investment tool in order to benefit from it. One of the exceptional things about Bitcoin is its ability to allow users to quickly and easily send money to each other across borders. If you need to send someone $1,500, for example, you could transfer that money into Bitcoins; send those coins to the appropriate wallet (we'll get into how exactly to do this a little later). You can also receive Bitcoins in the same manner. This is a way to use Bitcoin just as a quick tool, drop your money in, and take your money out.

- Long-Term Investment
  Another great way to use Bitcoin is as a form of long term investment. Most economists and forecasters agree that Bitcoin is here to stay, and it's only getting more and more legitimate as time goes on and interest builds. That demonstrates great long-term value. You may want to buy up Bitcoins when they're low every couple of weeks or months and store them in your wallet in hopes of keeping them for a long time. Five to ten years from now, the 17 Bitcoins that you paid $2,000 for could be worth $20,000 or more. You can also mix buying/selling Bitcoins with long term investment by periodically selling off Bitcoins when

the market is high, while keeping a store of Bitcoins for long term investment.

- Buying Stuff

    As previously discussed, a growing number of online and offline venues are accepting Bitcoin now as a form of payment. Later we'll explore the various places where you can use your Bitcoins.

Chapter 3:

How to mine Bitcoins Efficiently

Bitcoin mining is one of the fundamental aspects of the Bitcoin system that makes it what it is and makes it successful. To understand mining, you require to comprehend the open-source nature of the Bitcoin ledger. The Bitcoin system uses an open-source platform for maintaining transaction records, verifying them and preventing duplicate transactions from taking place. This system is basically a running record of all Bitcoin transactions, from the original block created by the inventor, to each and every last .00000001 BTC, which is the smallest increment of Bitcoin currently possible.

It is important to note that while Bitcoins are considered somewhat anonymous, the public nature of this ledger, known as the block chain, prevents real anonymity. This is because each transaction is recorded and open for everyone to see and verify, containing a unique identifier called a key, for each party of the transaction. The transactions, however, do not record the name of the persons or the goods or services being exchanged for Bitcoins.

The process of Bitcoin mining is simply doing the network the favor of verifying and authenticating previous Bitcoin transactions in exchange for a block of Bitcoins. Here is a brief explanation of how the mining process works, using three fictitious characters who we can call Jane, Bob, and Joe. Each of them has his or her wallet, and the free open source software needed to use them to conduct the transactions.

BITCOIN

Let's say that both Joe and Jane have something that Bob wants to purchase with one of his Bitcoins. Bob can post a transaction, called a block, to the network showing that he is giving a Bitcoin to either Joe or Jane, or he could post two transactions or blocks showing he is giving Joe and Jane each a separate Bitcoin, or even dishonestly post two transactions showing that he is giving the same Bitcoin to both Joe and Jane simultaneously. As mentioned earlier Bitcoin presumes to solve the problem of double spending, as Bob might attempt to do in the third example above.

In order to maintain the legitimacy of the transactions, the network uses third-party consensus to review and document only those transactions upon which everyone agrees are legitimate. So when Bob, Joe, and Jane announce their transactions to the network, the miners authenticate the transactions and broadcast back to the network whether they are legitimate or not. In order to do this, miners use powerful computing to solve a mathematical problem called a proof of work puzzle. By solving this, miners demonstrate that they have done the work of authenticating transactions.

In case of any disagreement, it is the miner that has done the most work that the network accepts as correct. In case Bob attempts to double spend his single coin, the miners on the network will notice that there are two pending transactions for the same coin, and notify all of the users this fact, including Joe and Jane, who would logically decline to accept Bob's offer, then that transaction is verified by the miners and made permanent in the Block chain.

To put it simply in a layman's; recent transactions are logged as pending on an open-source network, and kept in locked virtual boxes. The miners all try to find the key to the box, using their computing power to generate millions of virtual keys to the lock.

The lucky miner who finds the key first opens the lock and sends all of the transactions to the rest of the network for verification. As payment for doing this work, the miner who finds the key gets the reward of 25 Bitcoins.

What do you need to mine Bitcoins?

The software itself is free, consisting of a Bitcoin wallet and the mining software itself, so all you require is a computer that is capable of performing extremely fast calculations. The faster your computer is, the more likely you are to find the key needed to get the payout. In the late January 2014, it took on average 1.8 billion attempts to get the right key.

In the early days of Bitcoin, the average home computer was more than fast enough to mine Bitcoins profitably. When the number of transactions increased, so did the difficulty of mining, and thus the amount of computing power required to find the key for opening new blocks in the blockchain. As the number of transactions and miners increased, the standard CPU in a home computer ceased to be powerful enough to competitively mine and miners began using more powerful GPUs.

When the GPU was never competitive, miners turned to FPGA that is the Field-Programmable Gate Array. The use of the FPGA allowed miners to operate more efficiently when the value of Bitcoins took a dive in 2011. As the competition in the mining community increased, a new computing solution appeared on the scene that would appear to make the most efficient use of resources including power and time, the ASIC (application-specific integrated circuit) chip.

These chips are the first devices designed from the ground up for mining Bitcoins. At this time the waiting list and price of these high-power pieces of hardware is long and high, but the return on investment is as little as a couple of months with the potential for hundreds of US dollars in income per day, per unit. A spot in line on the waiting list for an ASIC has been known to sell on eBay for up to ten times the price of the ASIC itself, but the income potential for ASIC-equipped mining operations is great.

As the cost of running a mining operation increases, miners are finding new ways of making use of less-expensive hardware to mine Bitcoins by cooperatively pooling computing resources. A prospective Bitcoin miner can join a mining operation consisting of many GPUs or USB mining units independently owned and share the mining proceeds collectively with the other miners in the pool. A pool of 100 miners working to mine 25 Bitcoins a week would split the Bitcoins amongst themselves so that each miner receives 0.25 Bitcoins regardless of which miner owned the computer that found the right key.

As the technology and pool of Bitcoin miners continue to fluctuate, those interested in participating or investing in Bitcoin mining need to conduct diligent research on the most current methods and technology before entering the business of mining. Some way consider it a game and some may consider it a legitimate money-making opportunity and even others may consider it a waste of time, but thing is certain; those who successfully mine Bitcoins do stand to make a virtual ton of money.

Setting up an account

You can obtain a bitcoin wallet from a Bitcoin agent, for example, Coinbase. Once you open up a wallet through a guaranteed specialist, you are given a Bitcoin address which is a progression of numbers and letters, likewise to an account number for a financial balance and a private key which is a progression of numbers and letters also, which fill in as your secret key.

How to send Bitcoin

For you to pay for goods & services or to send bitcoins between individuals, three things are required. Your Bitcoin address, your private key & the person's bitcoin address. Starting there, through your Bitcoin wallet, you will put three snippets of data, which are: inputs, output, and balance. Input alludes to your address; balance alludes to the bitcoins you will send, and output is the beneficiary's address.

What are the different ways of storing Bitcoins?

Bitcoin is applauded for giving its clients full control over their assets, in the meantime, more control accompanies greater obligation to protect those assets. There are a wide range of approaches to secure your Bitcoins each having its own advantages and disadvantages. Here are some of the ways to store your Bitcoins some of which are common.

1. **Storing Bitcoins on an Exchange**
   The most well-known and simplest approach to store your Bitcoins is on an exchange. There are various exchanges accessible, look at various Bitcoin exchange charts to see which one may be ideal for you. Keep in mind however, that this method of storing Bitcoins is not prescribed for the basic reason that you don't have full control over your coins.

Exchanges can get hacked or shut your account down for some reason, and you could possibly lose every one of your assets. Not to state that exchanges don't have a place in the environment as they are extraordinary entrance ramps for starters to buy Bitcoins and get acquainted with the way towards utilizing them.

2. **Storing Bitcoins on an Online Wallet**

    A superior approach to store your Bitcoins would be storing on an online wallet. Blockchain.info & GreenAddress are recently a portion of a couple of alternatives accessible for online wallets, to discover the correct wallet for you look at various Bitcoin wallet comparison charts not forgetting about the reviews. Fortunately utilizing this method; you do have full control over your coins as you can separate the private keys from the wallets. In any case, the drawback is, that the private keys are likewise stored online which make them immune to hacks and potential zero-day exploitation. On the off chance that you are searching for a helpful approach to store your Bitcoins and are not very worried about utmost security, you should give online wallets a shot.

3. **Storing Bitcoins in a Desktop Wallet**

    A safer yet still helpful choice to store your Bitcoins is to utilize desktop wallets. Best of all, the private keys are just stored on your local machine, implying that presentation of the key online is insignificant. However, if your machine gets tainted with a Bitcoin taking malware, consider your coins gone. Moreover, contingent upon what desktop wallet arrangement you pick, and how you set it up, you can execute Bitcoins more secretly as your IP address, and Email won't be connected to the Bitcoin wallet dissimilar to if you somehow managed to utilize an online arrangement.

4. **Storing Bitcoins in a Mobile Wallet**

    Another quite secure way to store your Bitcoins is utilizing a portable wallet. Wallets, for example, Mycelium & Breadwallet are both extraordinary applications which you can download on your telephone's application store. The wallets don't require any individual data so you can be certain your exchanges are at any rate to some degree unknown. Beyond any doubt, the application will connect your telephones ID or IMEI, however in the event that the telephone is a burner, it is difficult to interface the wallet to a genuine personality. Moreover, online wallets store the keys on your telephone, and for the situation that your telephone is lost, you can simply utilize the given back up to regain your coins.

5. **Storing Bitcoins on a Hardware Wallet**

    A standout among the most secure approaches to store your Bitcoins is on the hardware wallets. Arrangements, for example, Trezor, KeepKey, & Ledger are generally extraordinary choices in the event that you are hoping to expand the security of your assets. Moreover, these wallets give a totally mysterious alternative to execute cryptocurrency. Since no individual data is connected to the gadget, there is no identifying information to leak. The reason these gadgets are so secure is that the keys are stored on a dedicated piece of hardware. Malware will have a hard time while attempting to move beyond the wallet's equipment security and take your coins. Moreover, much the same as whatever other wallets, you can undoubtedly recoup the assets with a seed expression in the event that the gadget is lost or broken.

6. **Storing Bitcoins on a Paper Wallet**

   Paper wallets aren't much popular as some different arrangements as they require much comprehension of the protocol. You can create a Bitcoin paper wallet at Bitcoinpaperwallet.com, which will manage you on the best way to accurately produce it. Besides, you can produce it offline for most extreme security by detaching your PC from the web while making it. Paper wallets can be stored at anyplace and don't consume much space. The advantage is this is a 100% unknown method for storing your coins as a paper wallet is basically a Bitcoin seed on a bit of paper. Besides, if the bit of paper is appropriately secured, there is no chance for programmers to take it as the wallet never touched the web in any case.

7. **Storing Bitcoins on a multi-signature Wallet**

   Another less normal approach to store your Bitcoins is on a Multisig wallet. A Multisignature wallet requires numerous individuals to endorse an exchange before it can happen. This would be an awesome answer for storing Bitcoins that have a place with various individuals, similar to an organization that has Bitcoin finance. Suppose you don't need a solitary individual to have control over your organization's assets; you could setup a signature wallet that would require different officials to approve an exchange before it can get endorsed.

8. **Burying your Bitcoins**

   Since we are finished with the more evident Bitcoin storage methods, we proceed onward to the fun ones. In case you are feeling additionally distrustful of somebody burglarizing your home or approaching your machine, you could print a paper wallet, or utilize a hardware wallet like Cryptosteel and cover your Bitcoins in your terrace or in the forested areas. For greater security, you could likewise reinforce the covered wallet on a paper wallet in the event that you cannot recall where you covered it.

9. **Storing Bitcoins on your body**

   Another inventive approach to store your Bitcoins is on your body. While it might sound peculiar in the first place, inking a 12-word seed, or if nothing else an expression or sentence which would enable you to recollect the seed could be a thought worth engaging. Clearly, on the off chance that somebody finds the seed subsequent to seeing your tattoo, it might render that seed pointless. It would presumably be best to make a kind of figure that you only know. Along these lines neither the tattooer nor whatever other individual seeing the tattoo can break its encryption.

10. **Storing Bitcoins in your Bank**

    While it might seem like the most exceedingly terrible thought conceivable, storing Bitcoin in your bank might be more secure than you might suspect. You could create a paper wallet and place it in your security store box. Along these lines, your Bitcoins are both safe from theft, and a house fire, however, they are additionally stored secretly without the bank knowing.

11. **Storing Bitcoins on Physical Coins**

    There are a couple of services out there which enable you to purchase physical Bitcoins. You buy this physical coin which contains a carefully designed sticker under which is a foreordained measure of Bitcoins. Physical coins make an incredible gatherer's thing and can be stored similarly one would store adornments or gold – either in a bank or in a safe. One issue with acquiring physical coins is the means by which you should pay a premium on the Bitcoins, for instance, a coin stacked with

$100 worth of Bitcoin may cost $150 or more. In addition, you should believe the organization issuing the coin to legitimately secure the private keys and not take the bitcoins later on at a future date.

12. **Storing the Bitcoins in plain sight**

    One of the most ideal approaches to store Bitcoins is on display. Steganography is the craft of disguising messages or data inside other non-secret content or information. One could shroud a Bitcoin private key inside a picture and put it on their wall. If somebody in some way happened to break into your home, taking a boring painting would be the last thing of their thoughts. Moreover, you could make it harder by scrambling the information in the picture with a passphrase, that way if somebody figures out you are concealing Bitcoins in a picture he would require the passphrase to get to them.

Chapter 4:

Bitcoin Exchanges

In this chapter, we will have an in-depth look at what Bitcoin exchanges are, how they work and what value they offer to the Bitcoin currency system. While Bitcoin was intended to function as a peer-to-peer (P2P) currency without the use of middlemen such as banks or exchanges, such entities do exist and operate within the Bitcoin system. Even though Bitcoin was designed not to need them, whenever a free market system has a demand, someone will fill that demand if the potential for profit is perceived to be high. So what drives the demand for exchanges in a system that was designed to operate without them?

For users to own and trade with Bitcoins, they need a place to store them. Since Bitcoin is a virtual currency, there are many places where they can be stored, including on a home computer. As the public transaction ledger, or blockchain, became larger with more and more transactions, storing Bitcoins on a home computer began to require more and more memory. The memory requirements being a result of having to update the block chain on the user's computer each time the user wanted to conduct a transaction.

While the use of a Bitcoin client on a home computer to store Bitcoins is the most secure method of storage, the increasing memory requirements became problematic for some. By using a Bitcoin exchange, users entrust the storage of their storage of their Bitcoins (and in some cases other funds) to a third party, who essentially operates as a bank for its users, or account holders.

Bitcoin exchanges are used for more than just storing Bitcoins. An exchange allows a user to connect his or her bank or credit card account to an exchange to which funds are transferred in any of some global currencies. Once a user has funded an exchange account, the funds can be used to purchase Bitcoins from another user, including the exchange itself. The exchange can hold the user's Bitcoins in a separate and private account until the account holder is ready to use them in conducting Bitcoin transactions.

Operating and/or using a Bitcoin exchange can be a complicated and even risky business. A reputable exchange needs to be able to offer account holders a high level of security and extremely accurate record-keeping. Account holders entrust an exchange with real-world bank or credit card account information for funding accounts with currencies like the US Dollar, British Pound, Japanese Yen, and many others.

The exchange also needs a secure and accurate means of exchanging its account holder's various currencies for Bitcoins at the proper exchange rate, and then assigning the exchanged Bitcoins to a secure account that only its account holder has access to, either an account with the exchange itself or the user's personal Bitcoin address. Users can then utilize their Bitcoin account or address to exchange Bitcoins for other currencies, goods, or services offered by others in the Bitcoin network, including many brick-and-mortar establishments as well as online entities.

While using an exchange can be risky, there are good exchanges available with solid reputations. When choosing to work with a Bitcoin exchange, it is critical for prospective account holders to conduct as much research as necessary to ensure that the exchange they are considering is known to be legitimate, offering guaranteed security to account holders that includes returning money from hacked accounts and fair market value compensation for stolen or lost Bitcoins.

Account holders should ensure that the identities and actual physical addresses of those owning and operating the exchange are known and confirmed. One of the best methods for researching an exchanging is to talk to other Bitcoins users, and to check feedback ratings for an exchange. Prospective account holders should be aware of the liquidity of the exchange, which is how quickly cash can be exchanged for Bitcoins and vice versa.

Liquidity is a major factor when it comes to trading Bitcoins for the sole purpose of making money by purchasing them for cash and selling them when their value increases. Legitimate exchanges with the best reputations are those that don't deny vulnerabilities or potential threats; rather they address them openly. In addition to Mt.Gox, some well-known exchanges include Slovenia-based Bitstamp, US-based CampBX, China-based BTC China, and Canada-based VirtEx.

Once you have selected an exchange, you will need to create an account. The better-known exchanges; and for that matter legitimate, will ask you for personal information such as a confirmed address, phone number, or even a scanned copy of your identification card to set up an account. As soon as you have an account, you are ready to buy and sell Bitcoins. Exchanges function, generally, in one of two ways. Some exchanges buy Bitcoins in bulk, or from account holders, at the lowest price they can find and then store them to offer for sale to account holders wishing to purchase them.

This type of exchange generally makes a profit by selling Bitcoins at a higher price than it purchased them. The second type of exchange is basically a type of match-making service. It simply uses its trading software to match prospective sellers, charging a small fee for the service. This type of exchange allows sellers to advertise their Bitcoins for sale at or above a certain maximum price. The exchange's software finds buyers who are willing to pay the minimum price asked for by the seller, and it also finds sellers willing to offer Bitcoins for the maximum price requested by the buyer.

When a match is found the parties either must agree to complete the transaction, after which the software transfers buyers' funds into sellers' accounts and sellers' Bitcoins into buyers' accounts or the transaction is automatically completed based on instructions specified by both buyers and sellers.

The business of operating a Bitcoin exchange can be quite lucrative for those familiar with the stock market and the way that stock trading software works. In fact, many exchanges are started and operated by stock trading veterans. The market volatility of the Bitcoin can be exploited by exchanges to buy low from bulk or individual sellers and sell high, just like a veteran stock trader would do on the NYSE.

Those not wishing to actually operate an exchange, but who are willing to undertake speculative risk in trading a volatile currency like Bitcoin, can utilize an exchange to buy Bitcoins at low prices from motivated sellers and sell them to the highest bidders on the same exchange for a profit. Historically, Bitcoin prices have been listed at widely varying prices on various exchanges; this is something that a prospective trader must keep in mind when choosing an exchange.

One may be better off with some accounts at separate exchanges than a single account at one exchange. As mentioned earlier, liquidity is key to making money by trading and multiple accounts can best serve traders in a market wherein some transactions may take days or weeks to convert Bitcoins into cash and vice versa. Generally speaking, however, the longer an account holder has held an account, and the more stable his or her history with an exchange is, the faster the exchange will process transactions.

Whether you want to enter the Bitcoin market to conduct regular business, to make investments, or to operate a business for a profit, the Bitcoin exchange can be a valuable tool and resource. Since there are very many of them, and due to the fact that they are diversely situated around the world, the current price of Bitcoins can vary significantly between exchanges. When prices between exchanges differ significantly enough, an arbitrage opportunity can exist.

Arbitrage is the practice of buying at low prices on one exchange and selling at another with higher prices. While this type of opportunity can happen often, it usually does not last long as arbitrage traders quickly cause prices to balance across the exchanges. One valuable resource for quickly checking prices at different exchanges can be found online at preev.com. This site is useful to anyone in the Bitcoin market, whether buying or selling Bitcoins.

Prices can be given in any of a number of world currencies including the US Dollar, the Euro, and the Canadian Dollar and up to 60 other world currencies. Preev also provides similar data for a number of other virtual currencies in addition to Bitcoins. Among the reasons as to why this site is so handy is that the users can easily select from 3 common denominations of Bitcoin: 1BTC, mBTC, and kBTC (mBitcoin=1/1000 of a Bitcoin, and kBitcoin=1000 Bitcoin) to see what the real-time conversion ratio is for any of the listed currencies.

The site is incredibly simple and easy to use: a user only selects the denomination of Bitcoin from a drop down menu, and can select from either of the more popular currencies or use a search field to find other currencies not shown on the menu. Users can even check Bitcoin prices against precious metals like gold, silver, and platinum. Depending on the currency selection, preev.com allows users to select data from all or any of the four different listed Bitcoin exchanges based overseas to determine current exchange rates.

Because Bitcoins are traded on many different exchanges, the current prices at each exchange can vary significantly. Sites like preev.com use real time data from multiple exchanges to compute an average, and there are some sites on the internet which can do these using even different exchanges. Users can combine data from multiple sites to compute their own averages as well.

To do so, users should keep in mind that each reported real-time average must be multiplied by the number of exchanges reporting, then summed with the same data from another Bitcoin reporting site, and then divided by the total number of exchanges. This may sound complicated, but it is really an easy way to keep track of the global average exchange rate rather than just looking at regional data.

Capital gains from Bitcoins and long term investing

Bitcoin can be a profitable investment in that they provide prospective investors a means of purchasing an asset that has the potential for an increase in value. Interestingly, Bitcoin has more than one fundamental contributing to this potential. We have briefly discussed two of the factors that contribute to Bitcoin's potential, the first being the fixed nature of the supply of Bitcoins. Unlike other currencies, Bitcoins cannot be simply printed or created at will. Bitcoins are created at a predictable, self-regulating, and pre-determined rate that puts a cap on the eventual Bitcoin supply.

As long as the Bitcoin has some intrinsic value, which is the service that it provides to its users (that is, the capacity to conduct easy and fast transactions online between anonymous and distant parties), with a fixed supply the value is likely to increase. The second factor contributing to a potential for an increase in value is the volatility of the currency itself. While volatility is difficult if not impossible to predict, it can be a reliable source of value increase that traders can use to make a great deal of money. Once Bitcoin started to really take off in 2011, one reliable trait has been its volatility.

Like trading in the stock market, volatility can bring huge gains to investors who are willing to take on the big risk, but could just as easily result in massive losses. What makes Bitcoin different is that it has steadily maintained an increase in value based on yearly averages, despite huge drops in value that are below the average price for given periods of time. Volatility does result in large crashes in price, but in the case of Bitcoin, each crash has generally bottomed out at a price that was higher than the price at the start of the upswing prior to the crash.

In other words, Bitcoin has behaved like a steadily growing but volatile tech stock: with periods of both bearish and bullish activity, each bull market has ended higher than the preceding bear market; indicative of steady growth. So how can a prospective investor capitalize on the potential for profit by buying and selling Bitcoins? One fundamental method involves the ability to identify trends in price.

We just mentioned one trend, that Bitcoin seems to be capable of ending its downswings higher than previous downswings, and the same is true with upswings in that the high points of the currency generally show greater gains than the previous period's high swings, indicating volatility but at the same time steady growth. This allows an investor to accept a certain amount of short-term risk due to the indications of long-term growth.

In addition to the history of long-term growth, Bitcoin may be capable of showing signs that are indicative of either up or down swings in value. An observant and vigilant investor may be able to identify key indicators that can point to future up or down swings, allowing that investor to trade in Bitcoins profitably. What are the major indicators of future swings in the price of Bitcoin? This is an important question to any prospective investor, whether investing in Bitcoins or in securities on the stock market.

Fortunately, Bitcoin investing seems to have a more predictable volatility than many stocks or other currencies. While it is predictable that an investment security or currency will decrease in value following adverse publicity and increase in value following good publicity, these indicators are not often well enough in advance to benefit many investors. In this case of Bitcoin, however, unlike publicly-traded securities, the entire history of Bitcoin transactions is available to the public.

Anyone with the right software, software that is openly available for free, can monitor transactions in real time. This gives prospective investors the ability to identify trading trends and Bitcoin transactions in real time. Bitcoins seem to predictably fall in value immediately following bad publicity as Bitcoin owners exchange their holdings for cash, and Bitcoins seem to reliably stabilize in value at a price that is higher than the previous lows.

Seemingly, all a Bitcoin investor needs to do to make money is to monitor the trading of Bitcoins during a down swing and purchase them when they begin to rebound in value. When the price of Bitcoin reaches a point that makes a profit for the investor, the investor can sell them for cash. While this process may sound overly simple, there are complications that an investor needs to be cognizant of. For one, trading in a volatile currency requires a great deal of market awareness.

One needs to know what type of news will result in the greatest price swings. One also needs to know that the previous highs and lows were, as well as how long each down and upswing period lasted. As with any investment, one also needs to know that past performance cannot be an indication of future performance and a wise investor needs to be capable of riding out downswings long enough for an investment to rebound.

Another key strategy is having multiple trading resources at your disposal. The time it takes to convert Bitcoins to cash can vary between exchanges, from less than 24 hours to several weeks. Exchanges are known to suspend trading due to extreme volatility or breaches in security. The worst thing an investor can do, aside from losing money, is to have funds or Bitcoins looked up in a frozen account while an exchange works out some bug in its systems.

In order to ensure liquidity and the ability to make fast trades when market conditions are right, an investor will need accounts with multiple Bitcoin exchanges. This allows an investor to use an alternate account to buy or sell Bitcoins at the current market price even when some exchanges suspend trading. The best advice for users wishing to start trading Bitcoins for a profit would be to use exchanges that you fully trust with your money and Bitcoins.

So how can you trust an exchange that operates overseas, in the midst of the rise and fall of dozens of exchanges, many of which have taken their account holders' coins and money with them when they fell? Beginners may want to start out with 2-3 different accounts at different exchanges, so be prepared to do some research. One resource is Bitcointalk.org an online forum where users discuss the different aspects of doing business with, trading, and making money with Bitcoins.

Forums like this are a good way to find out which exchanges are recommended by other users, and which are not. Remember, exchanges are subject to regulations imposed by the countries in which they operate, which can regularly change. This means that what may have been the best exchange six months ago may no longer be. Beginners will want an exchange with low fees, low commissions, the simplest trading platform, and security.

All of these factors are subject to revision so beginners should always review them to update their choice of exchanges. It would make good sense to start out with a very simple exchange for making necessary long term trades, a high-speed trading exchange for more daily trading activity, and secure exchange for storing Bitcoins and other funds. Exchanges based in the United States may offer more security than those overseas.

Chapter 5:

Bitcoin real life usage

Bitcoins are a decentralized form of cryptocurrency. Meaning, they are not controlled by any financial organization or the legislature. In that capacity, dissimilar to a conventional bank account, one needn't bother with an insignificant list of printed material, for example, an ID in order for him or her to build up what's known as a bitcoin wallet. The bitcoin wallet is what you will need to get to your bitcoins and to send bitcoins to different people. Here are some of the Bitcoin real life usages:

Bitcoin Casino & the Poker Sites

Because of the anonymous nature of bitcoin, the betting business has taken up Bitcoin as a payment technique. Both Bitcoin casinos & Bitcoin poker sites are being revived and offering their players to deposit, play with the Bitcoin at the tables and pull back quickly to their Bitcoin wallet. This implies there are no duties or likely outcomes for government control. Just as a standard Nevada casino where you don't need to register anywhere and all your transactions are anonymous.

Bitcoin as an Anonymous Payment Processor

You can perform three things using bitcoins; you can purchase, send cash anonymously to somebody or use it as an investment. An ever increasing number of shippers have been tolerating bitcoins as a type of installment. By utilizing bitcoins rather than money, you are basically making the purchase anonymously. A similar thing applies when sending cash, in light of the way that you don't need to present a pile of payment in order to build up a Bitcoin secretly. Basically, you can send money to someone else anonymously.

Bitcoin as an Investment

The price of a Bitcoin changes occasionally. Just to place things in context, back toward the start of 2013, the normal price of a Bitcoin was roughly $400 per bitcoin, yet before the end of 2013, the price of Bitcoin again rose to over $1000. This implied on the off chance that you had two bitcoins worth $800 toward the start of 2013 and you put it away as a venture before the end of 2013, those two bitcoins would have been worth over $2000 rather than $800. Many individuals store bitcoins on the grounds that its value vacillates.

The Reasons why you should Use Bitcoin

Why utilize Bitcoin? What are its advantages? Why is it superior to money or credit cards? These are questions that are always asked. Regardless of the fast price swings, or maybe to some extent as a result of them, Bitcoin has increased impressive notoriety among a wide range of financial specialists, from speculative stock investments to tech-billionaires to general individuals hoping to grow their funds. Below is a quick list of reasons why you, or anyone, will find Bitcoin to be beneficial to have and use and why they should consider including it in their portfolio.

1. It is made for our era
   What we simply mean by that is that Bitcoin is made for the Internet era. We are rapidly moving past the times of bearing paper money or hauling out your credit card. Bitcoin goes a few stages more remote than the comfort of credit cards by furnishing clients with a payment alternative that is necessarily lower in charges, gives

basically momentary exchange time, and is available through the many Bitcoin wallets. Other than convenience, Bitcoin offers card clients opportunity from the worries of misrepresentation, data fraud, and devastating interest rates.

2. It is quick, secure & worldwide
   Bitcoin doesn't segregate. One can utilize it at anyplace on the planet, to send value immediately, almost free. Exchanging bitcoins costs only a couple of pennies and you can send as much value as you need. It's critical to recall that bitcoins can't be falsified or copied. The incredible fact is that exchanges are led in a distributed technique, without the requirement for a bank or an outsider to supervise it.
3. Bitcoin was planned in light of your security
   The Bitcoin piece adventurers show the whole history of Bitcoin exchanges for all to see. Bitcoin exchange history can be looked by anybody with access to the internet. At first look, you should seriously think about this level of openness the inverse of private. In actuality, it implies that clients can pick whether they need to be totally transparent with their accounts or keep them exceptionally private. The Bitcoin convention does not expect individuals to identify themselves so as to transact; however, a few organizations may need to for compliance purposes. Not at all like a bank where individuals frequently may have a couple of accounts, you can make many Bitcoin wallets as you like.
4. Bitcoin is not a subject to inflation
   The aggregate number of bitcoins is topped at 21 million, which is unique in relation to different monetary

standards. As the total number of dollars available for use rises, this constitutes some inflation. This is the place the estimation of your dollar, for instance, diminishes after some time because of an expanding supply. Bitcoin, then again, is rare and fungible, which gives it remarkable properties.

5. Bitcoin gives a budgetary flexibility

   On the off chance that you don't have a bank account, you are a piece of the "unbanked." Bitcoin can enable you to be your own bank. Bitcoin is an open financial convention & a currency required so as to execute properly on the convention.

6. Irreversible exchanges

   The irreversibility of exchanges makes buyer to vendor extortion close to impossible. This has exceptional applications. There are a few regions in the conventional economy where purchaser to trader fraud is widespread... for example, the offering of virtual merchandise and presumably pornography. Some contend that it is a terrible thing. However, the truth of the matter is that it is ideal to have irreversibility with the choice to have reversibility on top than it is to have just reversibility with no irreversibility choice.

7. Money related power

   Humanity has never truly possessed their cash. It's dependably been claimed by their rulers. Bitcoin gives the capacity for individuals to really claim their own particular cash. You can't in any way, shape or claim something if another person can weaken its value by making more & taking it from you through inflation. With Bitcoin, the sum that will be made is known, and that's it.

BITCOIN

8. The borderless factor
   Presently, most cash needs to move customarily through moderate, lumbering frameworks that can commonly include vast charges on top. With bitcoin, anybody could be paid, and there are no outskirts or limits. This unquestionably has benefits in numerous ranges... settlement for instance. The investment funds would be much more noteworthy on account of the settlement if Bitcoin was utilized all the more generally and didn't should be changed over to different monetary standards at each end. Capital controls are another zone that fit under this element. A few nations need to restrict where you can send your cash so they can keep your riches inside the nation. However, perhaps you simply need to clear out?
9. A place of refuge from bank emergencies
   Cash in the bank is not as secure as it used to be. In Cyprus, savers saw an irregular demand taking a huge "hair style" off the estimation of their retirement funds, while the general population of Greece is enduring expanded breaking points on the measure of money they can withdraw from their banks. Cryptocurrency does not only exclusively give a place of refuge from these dangers, yet it additionally enables you to benefit from the expanded profit produced when things like this happen.
10. Immediate access
    You don't necessarily need to tie up cash in long haul designs keeping in mind the end goal to make some profit. As a type of cash itself, this is a venture you can get to in a flash whenever.

Limitations of Bitcoin

Bitcoin is cash like no other. To put it plainly, it's advanced cash that tackles a significant number of the issues our present monetary forms experience the ill effects of and presents numerous different instabilities we never needed to manage. Like any money, there are impediments related with utilizing Bitcoin:

1. **Bitcoins are not broadly acknowledged**
   Bitcoins are still just acknowledged by a little gathering of online traders. This makes it unfeasible to totally depend on Bitcoins as cash. There is additionally a plausibility that administrations may drive vendors to not utilize Bitcoins to guarantee that clients' exchanges can be easily tracked.
2. **Wallets can be lost**
   In the event that a hard drive crashes or an infection ruins information, and the wallet document is tainted, Bitcoins have basically been "lost." There is nothing that should be possible to recuperate it. These coins will be everlastingly stranded in the system. This can bankrupt a well off Bitcoin speculator in a matter of seconds with no chance of recuperation. The coins the financial specialist claimed will likewise be permanently stranded.
3. **Bitcoin valuation varies**
   The estimation of Bitcoins is always fluctuating based on the demand. This consistent variance will cause Bitcoin accepting sites to always change prices. It will likewise cause a considerable measure of perplexity if a discount for an item is being made. For instance, if a shirt was at first purchased for 1.5 BTC, and restored seven days after the fact, should 1.5 BTC be returned, despite the fact that the valuation has gone up, or should the new sum (ascertained by current valuation) be sent? Which cash

should BTC attach to when looking at valuation? These are as yet imperative inquiries that the Bitcoin users still have no accord over.

4. **No buyer assurance**
   At the point when products are purchased utilizing Bitcoins, and the vendor doesn't send the agreed merchandise, there is no hope to turn around the exchange. This issue can be unraveled utilizing an outsider escrow benefit yet at that point; escrow administrations would accept the part of banks, which would make Bitcoins be like a more customary currency.

5. **Danger of obscure technical defects**
   The Bitcoin framework could contain unexploited flaws. As this is a generally new framework, if Bitcoins were received broadly, and a defect was discovered, it could give colossal riches to the exploiter to the detriment of devastating the Bitcoin economy.

6. **Built in deflation**
   Since the aggregate number of bitcoins is topped at 21 million, it will cause flattening. Each bitcoin will be worth more as the total number of Bitcoins maximizes. This framework is intended to remunerate early adopters. Due to the fact that each bitcoin will be valued higher with each passing day, the subject of when to spend ends up noticeably vital. This may cause spending surges which will cause the Bitcoin economy to change quickly, and unusually.

7. **No physical form**
   Since Bitcoins don't have a physical frame, it can't be utilized as a part of physical stores. It would dependably be changed over to different monetary forms. Cards with

Bitcoin wallet data stored in them have been proposed, yet there is no accord on a specific framework. Since there would be numerous contending frameworks, dealers would think that it is unfeasible to help all Bitcoin cards, and along these lines, clients would be compelled to convert Bitcoins at any rate, unless an all comprehensive framework is proposed and actualized.

8. **No valuation assurance**
    Since there is no focal authority representing Bitcoins, nobody can ensure its base valuation. In case a vast gathering of vendors chooses to "dump" Bitcoins and leave the framework, its valuation will diminish considerably which will massively hurt clients who have a lot of riches invested into Bitcoins. The decentralized idea of bitcoin is both a revile and gift.

9. **There is no national bank for Bitcoin**
    Without a doubt, there never will be one, on the grounds that Bitcoin's avoidance of central control requests to its clients. A national bank oversees partial hold loaning that enables a national economy to grow. The supply of cryptocurrency is constrained by an algorithmic plan, so an economy running on Bitcoin can't extend to suit a bigger populace or characteristic asset base. A Bitcoin economy can't develop on the grounds that it can't send abundance capital for innovation.

Chapter 6:

Bitcoin Security tips and safety features

Bitcoin has certainly revolutionized the way people do business payment transactions today. This crypto currency was created in 2009 by someone bearing the pseudonym Satoshi Nakamoto. With this type of currency, the transactions are often made with no middle men, which means there would be no bank involved and the government will not be involved either.

As such, there will not be any transaction fees to pay and no need to give out your actual name & other personal information. Despite these advantages, the Bitcoins also come with security shortcomings and if you are not aware of the Bitcoin security and safety tips you could end up being a victim.

These days, you will find that more and more merchants are beginning to accept Bitcoins as a mode of payment. You can purchase web hosting services using your Bitcoins. You can buy pizza using this, and you can even get a manicure with this currency.

Payments made using Bitcoins are almost instantaneous. There' no credit card that needs to be processed. There's no lengthy verification and above all, there won't be any hidden fees for every transaction.

Also, using Bitcoins for international payments is cheaper since they are not tied to any country and is not subject to any government regulation. Small businesses love the fact that there are no fees for using this crypto currency and that's why you can find a lot of them using Bitcoins in doing business now.

There are even others who make money out of it, by buying Bitcoins as their investment and selling them at a later time once the value goes up. But then, there are also some drawbacks that come with using Bitcoins and if there's one major weakness, it's the Bitcoin security and safety.

When you have Bitcoins, you store them in your own Bitcoin wallets. In effect, you are your own bank. If in case you encrypt your wallet and you happen to forget the pass key, your Bitcoins will be gone forever and there is no way of recovering it.

There are also instances that hackers and scammers would be able to get access to your Bitcoins. In some cases, a malware virus will get to it and whatever Bitcoins you have in your wallet will all be gone in seconds. Remember that if your Bitcoins will be lost, there is no one you can turn to.

As mentioned, you are your own bank, so unlike a traditional way of banking where your money is covered by insurances, with Bitcoins, there is none. But this is not to scare you, if ever you are planning to be part of the Bitcoin network. This is only to inform you of the importance of Bitcoin security and safety. Indeed, security and safety are of utmost importance when transacting with Bitcoins so below are some factors that you should remember when it comes to securing your Bitcoins.

Do not use web wallets

A web wallet is also known as a hosted wallet because this is a type of Bitcoin wallet which is hosted by a third party. It's like entrusting your Bitcoins to another company. Although they may be easier to use, not all of them can provide a higher level of security to all the Bitcoins you have given them to be stored.

Once you decide to make use of this wallet, you will need to sign up for an account and you can then start to deposit your Bitcoins to your account. Once you have Bitcoins on your account, you can start buying the things you want using it and you can even send and receive Bitcoins through the web wallet.

But then, these web wallets are a magnet for hackers and therefore, they should be avoided as much as possible. But if it is essential to use one, then do your research well and choose the company that can provide the highest level of Bitcoin security and safety. You can read reviews online from other Bitcoin users who have tried using the web wallet. Also, you can choose to transfer your Bitcoins from your exchange based wallets after every exchange transaction. You can store it on your own personal computer and should be kept encrypted.

Limit the access to corporate Bitcoin wallets

You probably run a business and you have decided to use Bitcoins as your medium of currency. But be very careful with giving access to your Bitcoin wallets. This is very important in a corporate environment. Due to the anonymous nature of every Bitcoin transaction, it can be hard to trace if ever someone will attempt to steal your Bitcoins. If ever an employee would get access to your Bitcoin wallet, he or she can easily transfer the funds to another wallet without your knowledge. There is no way of tying the destination wallet to any individual employee.

For organizations that have several employees and staff and that some of the employees need access to the Bitcoin wallet in order to make certain transactions, it is recommended to make use of a wallet that comes with multiple sub wallets. You should be able to assign one sub wallet for every employee who will need to have access to your Bitcoins and make sure that each sub wallet should be protected with encryptions. This is among the most crucial Bitcoin security and safety tips to remember.

Separate your bitcoins to hot and cold wallets

Wallets that stay on machines which are connected to the World Wide Web are called hot wallets, since they are at high risk for network based attacks, as opposed to wallets that are offline in nature. If you are running any kind of Bitcoin online business, offline wallets will be a better tool. They are way safer and they are not that attractive to hackers. If you really need to make use of web based wallets, try to keep some of your Bitcoins on an offline wallet, or a cold wallet.

It would be ideal to keep the bulk of your Bitcoin funds on the offline wallet or the cold wallet. This can be stored in a safety deposit box if you prefer. Then you can keep just a small float of your Bitcoins on your online wallet or web wallet and this is what you are going to use for your day to day Bitcoin transactions. If in any case you will receive a huge amount of Bitcoins on your online wallet, move them as fast as possible to your offline wallet before the hackers could attack.

Store private keys offline

Another major Bitcoin security and safety tip that any Bitcoin user should remember is to keep private keys offline. As you know,

Bitcoin wallets would make use of public keys for sending and receiving Bitcoins. The public keys are also used for other functions such as checking your Bitcoin account balances. It is also the public keys that you will use to authorize payments from your Bitcoin wallets. Therefore, if anyone would be able to have access to your private keys, they can pretty much use your Bitcoins in whatever way they want without your knowledge.

In order to enhance the security of your Bitcoin wallet, remove its private keys and then store them somewhere, perhaps, in a separate computer that is not connected to the Internet. This way, you can be sure that it will not be compromised by hacker or malware attacks.

When making a payment of a transaction that is generated online, bring it to the offline computer with the use of a USB stick, and when it's already on the offline computer, that's when you enter the private key. After that, bring it back to your online computer and then complete the transaction there.

You may find this inconvenient but this is actually for your Bitcoin security and safety. Doing this will undoubtedly provide significant extra protection to your wallet. Remember, it is imperative that you keep your wallet protected especially if your wallet contains a lot of Bitcoins. Compromising a cold wallet is very difficult since it would require physical access.

Use a dedicated hardware

Make use of a dedicated hardware for doing your Bitcoin transactions. You can use a dedicated USB key in moving data from your online computer to your offline computer. This is to minimize its exposure to potential viruses. It will also help if you dedicate your offline computer exclusively for your offline wallet. This will also contribute to minimizing its potential exposure to viruses and web hackers.

Use Linux on online and offline computers

The best way to move data in between online and offline computers is to make use of a USB drive. This is also for your Bitcoin security and safety. Linux has the best record of resisting any USB based attacks so choose this as the USB drive for transferring Bitcoin related transactions from online to offline computers.

Keep a highly secure offsite backup

If your computer accidentally gets lost or stolen, or perhaps it got destroyed, and your hard disk fails to function, then you will no longer be able to have access to your wallet and most especially the Bitcoins that are on the wallet. This is the reason why Bitcoin experts would recommend that you back up your Bitcoin wallet elsewhere. One of the most useful Bitcoin security and safety tip is to create multiple backups that are stored in different locations.

Based on the type of wallet which you will use, you might be able to back up your wallet after every transaction or right after every 100 transactions in order to keep it updated with the latest private keys that have been made so as to have access to your Bitcoins.

Make use of a type 2 deterministic wallet

The biggest benefit of Type 2 Deterministic Wallet, which is a feature found on both Armory and Electrum open source wallets, is that it makes use of a seed in order to deterministically produce all of the future private keys for any of the Bitcoins that you have received. This implies that you will only need to create one backup server.

The reason behind this is because the backup has the seed. So if ever you lose your wallet accidentally, you can basically create a new wallet using that same seed, and your lost wallet will immediately be recreated with all of the private keys as well as the Bitcoins that were inside it.

Make use of fragmented backups

Although you might only need to create one backup for your seed ever, it is still recommended that you create multiple copies of such backup and then store them at various locations. If you are concerned with the physical security of your backup, then create a fragmented backup. This will split the seed into six fragments and any four will need to recreate the seed. You can then store each fragment in various locations. Before a thief could get access to your wallet, he would need first to have access to the four of the six fragments which are somehow difficult to him. The Armory wallet is one of the web wallets that provide the option of fragmented backups.

Make use of hardware wallet

A hardware wallet is also highly recommended if you are after the Bitcoin security and safety. This wallet effectively makes use of a USB key that comes with an on board computer running in its own special operating system, which is dedicated to operating a Bitcoin wallet.

A good example of this type of wallet is the Trezor. Its hardware can store the private keys of your Bitcoin wallets and will never divulge them. It works the same way as other laptop computer's TPM or Trusted Platform Module, which holds encryption keys.

By merely inserting a hardware wallet to an online machine, all Bitcoin transactions can be signed with the use of private keys that are stored in the hardware. Even if the online computer gets infected with malware and other viruses, Bitcoins will still be able to securely send and receive funds without getting access to all of the important private keys.

Bitcoin is an entirely new, unprecedented and sophisticated technology. Over time we will develop better security tools and practices that are easier to use by non-experts. Currently, Bitcoin users can use many of the tips above to enjoy a secure and trouble-free Bitcoin experience.

Chapter 7:

What's next for Bitcoins and other cryptocurrencies?

Current events, speculation, and volatility

There are a few reasons why cryptocurrencies are so intrinsically well known. They are secure, unknown and absolutely decentralized. Not at all like traditional money, they are not controlled or directed by some particular specialist; their flow is resolved completely by the market demands. They are likewise nearly difficult to fake; this is made possible by the complicated framework that encodes every last exchange, guaranteeing complete secrecy and express security to every single client. They even make for a really fulfilling, if unsafe, investment trial, in spite of the way that any monetary guide in their true personality will alert you to them. In this way, regardless of the actual high stakes that this kind of managing involves, also the absence of any administration organization to loan confidence to them, digital forms of money can just flourish and multiply.

There is much money to be made by using the Bitcoin market similar to how speculators use commodities, futures, and securities options. While opening your own Bitcoin businesses, trading site or exchange can be lucrative, there are already many of those services on the web and making a name yourself can be difficult. However, if you have a good grasp of the financial news, and how current events can impact the stock market, you can use that as a strategy for making money by speculating on the future price of Bitcoins. Speculators make money by buying something that is believed to be subject to significant increase in value, generally over a specified period of time, or by buying contracts to buy or sell something at a later date. Maintaining an awareness of what factors can affect future prices can be affected by such factors is instrumental to speculator's ability to profit from price changes.

It seems inevitable that Bitcoins will be subject to future regulations that will be imposed by governments of countries that have citizens using Bitcoins for more of their online transactions. Undoubtedly the impact of such future regulations will be evident in the market price of Bitcoins. Because they are traded on a number of exchanges that are based in different countries, the price impact is bound to vary at each of the various exchanges.

Speculators wishing to profit from the price swings after the imposing of new regulations will need to observe prices as news of government regulations are announced. There are likely to be two different types of new rules; those that restrict the trading of Bitcoins and that are intended to generate tax revenue for governments, and those that aim to protect the users themselves.

Each of these two types of regulations is likely to have a different short term and long term effects on the pricing. News of regulation may have the immediate effect of motivating Bitcoin owners to liquidate their coins in anticipation of a short term price decrease. As such a sell-off dies down and prices start to stabilize, buyers are generally encouraged to buy Bitcoins at the lower prices thus generating a market demand that will result in eventually higher prices.

News of regulation that is intended to protect users may have a small initial effect of decreasing prices while encouraging a long term increase in price. Speculation takes practice, and practiced, successful speculators are not afraid to act decisively upon either hearing news or in anticipation of news.

Currently, the future of Bitcoins is unknown and questionable at best. However, compared to other virtual currencies, Bitcoin seems to have been adequately designed to resist many of the vulnerabilities that have caused the downfall of its predecessors.

While there have been attempts at double spending, the open nature of the transaction record, the blockchain, has generally prevented double spending attempts from being successful. One need only to be in the habit of waiting for the 10-minute average that it takes for a block of transactions to be verified before accepting a Bitcoin trade or attempting to trade or trying to trade Bitcoins that have been recently received. The cases in which Bitcoins have been stolen or lost can generally be blamed on the lack of vigilance or due diligence on the party suffering the loss.

Bitcoin is based on open-source technology, which allows any user to add to, modify, or benefit the system and its users as a whole tend to be accepted while those that don't tend to be rejected. This process is decentralized, allowing for a consensus of users to agree or disagree on whether or not a change is beneficial to the system and its users. Those who attempt to abuse or cheat the system are generally quickly caught by the numerous legitimate users and flushed out before any real harm can be done.

So what exactly does the future of Bitcoin look like? If the past is any indication, results could be mixed. Most of the previous virtual currencies have failed. However, Bitcoin seems to have addressed the cause of past failures. Bitcoins own history has brought it from a virtual novelty, 10,000 of which could be traded for a pair of pizzas in 2010, to one that 10,000 of which could buy a multi-million dollar mansion in 2014.

While Bitcoin encountered a drop in its prices, a less expensive cryptocurrency by the name of Ether achieved its unequaled highs at $40 a unit. While Ether's present setup keeps it from being utilized as an immediate technique for payment, the digital currency still appears to have a brilliant future ahead because of the idea of savvy contracts. Meanwhile, more protection concerned digital money options are beginning to pick up noticeable quality for foundations, for example, Bitcoin, which in spite of their keen safety efforts, keep on having loop holes that could be misused for access to individual information.

We have seen already that with each rise and fall seems to bottom out higher than the previous low, and the point of stability appears to end up greater than the past as well. Expert opinions are mixed on the future of Bitcoin as well. It is perceived that Bitcoin will change the future of online buying and selling. This is because Bitcoin is a technological breakthrough that will last therefore continuing to make it easier and cheaper to buy and sell on the internet.

Other people argue that Bitcoin is too speculative in nature to last. This is due to the fact if more people are investing in Bitcoins as they believe that they will increase in value, and then fewer people will be spending them making them less valuable as a currency. These experts could be right or wrong, but that does not mean that investing in Bitcoins won't pay off.

Another factor that may drive the future of Bitcoin is government regulation. Currently, Bitcoin is largely unregulated as it is decentralized. No one government or bank has control over it. Thus its value is protected from inflation and is market driven. Some governments have publicly made statements concerning the legitimacy of Bitcoin as a currency, but those statements are likely subject to change as Bitcoin becomes more and more a mainstream form of currency.

Unlike other currencies other currencies, the Bitcoin supply is fixed and can't be increased. Bitcoins are provided at a predictable rate which will slow until production stops altogether. Other factors aside, this will result in an increase in the value of the future Bitcoins. As the difficulty of mining increases, we may see a consolidation of mining efforts into just a handful of mining operations that will reap all of the rewards of mining. What will happen if this occurs? What will the impact be on the accuracy and trustworthiness of the block chain? Theoretically, as the reward for mining decreases, and thus the number of miners, there will be less incentive for voluntary third-party verification of blocks of transactions.

If this happens, the legitimacy of Bitcoin will decrease. However, the business of verifying transactions can continue to be sufficiently profitable to encourage enough participation to keep the process honest. When the reward for mining Bitcoins is too small to be profitable, the transaction fees themselves should increase enough to motivate third parties to verify transactions.

Will cryptocurrencies be the new standard after 2017? Maybe it is too early to tell. However, if there is one thing we know without a doubt, it is that the cash appears to have a wide interest in a particular segment of innovatively wise people, a point that is certain to soon work to its support. Whether Bitcoin is here to stay for a long time, or it is destined to fail the next reduction in the mining reward in 2017, the time to make money with Bitcoins is none other than now.

Conclusion

Our voyage into the Bitcoin world brings profits from all corners. Fiscally, we can go through less on exchanges with Bitcoins while seeing our capacity to purchase items increment with the expansion in Bitcoin's value. The value increments are not apparently guaranteed. Also, our privacy will turn out to be practically invulnerable on the off chance that we pick that course.

Bitcoins and Bitcoins exchanging have accomplished large development in a record time. At the point when Bitcoins were first presented, there were many instances of extortion and instability, principally in light of the fact that most informal investors didn't know whether Bitcoins would stand the trial of time. Today, the Bitcoin exchange and mining field have developed to a point where extortion is practically unfathomable, and the exchange is as relentless as money markets. This development carries with it numerous open doors for the individuals who are quick to extend their feet in the lucrative trade.

We can make an online business that accepts Bitcoins with no bother, for example, charges and entanglements we would experience attempting to acknowledge credit cards. Notwithstanding managing the minor disturbance of adopting new terms and ideas appears like a little price to pay for the jackpot of advantages Bitcoin conveys. Far away however fundamentally vital is the future fortune Bitcoin guarantees to convey.

Bitcoin is quite literally changing the world. Although it's too early to tell the future for certain, one thing is for sure – cryptocurrency isn't going anywhere. Whether we see people with Bitcoin fifty to a hundred years from now is still yet to be seen. However, it is true that Bitcoin has paved the way for a new people's currency – not one confined by location or government or central bank, but one that crosses borders and all cultures.

Just like how the Internet has already changed the way people can get information and communicate with each other on a global level – a change that will most likely last forever – Bitcoin is now changing the way our economy works, how we pay for things, and how we regulate currency. The Internet opened everything up for us – it allowed us free access to as much information as we wanted, breaking the monopoly that formal education institutions had on the control of information, allowing anyone anywhere to learn anything at any time. It's a communal aspect of sharing and knowledge and change that has forever changed our culture for the better. It's only natural that the following step in that process is a new currency born out of such a revolutionary game changer as Internet.

Although Bitcoin may seem scary for a lot of people or may be initially confusing, it's always better to embrace it. Just as things like email and web browsing and online video and online banking and smart phones seemed scary and new at first, once these technologies were embraced, it no doubt added value to your life. So, don't be afraid of Bitcoin, embrace it now and be a part of the world's first ever decentralized digital currency, and a new dawn in how we think of money.

The aim of this book was to make you fully equipped in order to begin capitalizing on the Bitcoin "gold rush" which is currently occurring all around the world. As stated in the introduction, there is a lot of money on the table here for you to capture with Bitcoins. What will differentiate you from everyone else trying to get rich from this new form of currency is doing your homework, keeping on top of the exchanges and the mining hardware so that you can be ahead of the curve and leave the others in your dust. It is strongly advised to take the information presented in the book to begin your journey with Bitcoins and start your path towards financial freedom.

www.ingramcontent.com/pod-product-compliance
Lightning Source LLC
Chambersburg PA
CBHW050017230526
45470CB00003B/1008